Not by Bread Alone

Daily Reflections for Lent 2018

Michelle Francl-Donnay

LITURGICAL PRESS

Collegeville, Minnesota

www.litpress.org

Nihil Obstat: Reverend Robert Harren, *Censor deputatus*

Imprimatur: ✛ Most Reverend Donald J. Kettler, J.C.L.,
  Bishop of Saint Cloud, Minnesota, June 20, 2017.

Cover design by Monica Bokinskie. Photo courtesy of Thinkstock.

ISSN: 1552-8782

ISBN: 978-0-8146-4604-5   978-0-8146-4628-1 (ebook)

Introduction

Last fall my students and I walked part of the Kumano Kodo, an ancient network of pilgrimage trails in rural Japan. The terrain was rough and wildly overgrown, the paths sometimes edging along steep cliffs. We learned to keep a sharp eye for the stones marking the trail to avoid wandering off the track.

The psalms and scriptural texts laid out for Lent mark a pilgrimage through time rather than space, walking us through the high points of God's relationship with his people. They encourage us to explore the history of our own relationship with God. Where have I missed the markers on the way, and what experiences have taken my breath away?

I encourage you particularly to pray with the psalms. These were the poem-prayers that Jesus turned to in his own life and ministry. Psalm 37, verse 11 rings out in the Beatitudes near the start of Matthew's gospel: "But the poor will inherit the earth, / will delight in great prosperity." Christ's last words on the cross come from Psalm 22: "My God, my God, why have you abandoned me?" Listen to the psalms as they are sung. Search out different musical settings. Try Gregorio Allegri's shattering version of Psalm 51, which is the first psalm sung in Lent and the last on Holy Saturday night, or the same psalm set to the chant tones of Joseph Gelineau, SJ, sung by an English boys' choir. Pray them aloud, too, letting the Word that is God breathe in you.

There is a beauty as well as a wildness to Lent's path. God tells Israel in Isaiah, "I lay your pavements in carnelians, / your foundations in sapphires" (54:11). The readings marking our way along the days of the Lenten season are indeed like gemstones. Build your Lent around them, lay your life on their foundations, and together let us follow them on toward Easter.

Reflections

February 14: Ash Wednesday

A Time to Notice

Readings: Joel 2:12-18; 2 Cor 5:20–6:2; Matt 6:1-6, 16-18

Scripture:
"Take care not to perform righteous deeds
in order that people may see them . . . " (Matt 6:1a)

Reflection: "Do you know you have something on your forehead?" wonders the student in the front row of my general chemistry class. Inwardly, I wince, hearing again the morning's gospel: "when you fast, / . . . wash your face, / so that you may not appear to be fasting." Another student nudges her and whispers, "It's Ash Wednesday."

Every year I struggle with this paradoxical start to Lent, with the what and the why of Lenten penitence. None of this is required today. I was not obliged to go to Mass, or to let the gritty ashes be rubbed on my forehead. I could have taken the gospel to heart and washed my face before I went to class. Yet I have chosen to wear my faith—my penitence— on my face today, knowing there will be whispered "whys" swirling around my classroom.

Perhaps I am torn because I recognize Lent is a time of noticing, rather than being noticed. To stand back, sit down, empty out, and notice why and how I pray, where I am needed, who I should be.

"Why?" asks Jesus in the gospel. Why do you pray, fast, give alms? To be noticed? To be applauded? To be witness? Or to become? To become the face of Christ to your neighbor.

Lent calls us beyond the giving up of small luxuries, or even necessities, but through that emptying of ourselves and that carrying of others to become Christ. "Where is their God?" cried those who saw Israel's travails in the first reading. God is among us, in our neighbors, in our hearts. Would that you could read that on my face every day.

Meditation: What do you notice about the ways in which the gospel rubs against your everyday life? How might your Lenten practices make smooth those edges, let God be more apparent in you? Who might God be calling you to become this Lent?

Prayer: Merciful and compassionate God, open our hearts so that we might recognize your son in each other's faces, and in our own. Make known to us the paths we must walk, and sustain us in our Lenten journeys.

Whose Life Do I Choose?

Readings: Deut 30:15-20; Luke 9:22-25

Scripture:
  "I have set before you life and death,
  the blessing and the curse.
Choose life . . . " (Deut 30:19b)

Reflection: The choices set before me on any given day rarely seem as weighty as what Moses is offering the people of Israel. Chicken or fish for dinner tonight? White shirt or black turtleneck? Neither seems the stuff of life and death, a blessing or a curse—though admittedly it's a blessing to entertain such choices at all, to have clothes to wear, food in the freezer, enough and more to sustain my life.

Given so much and facing truly inconsequential choices, it is easy for me to think as I listen to the first reading that yes, I long ago chose life and its blessings, then plunge into my daily round of teaching and housework. Yet as I listen this morning, I hear the choice I make is not just for me, but has consequences for others. Choose life, cries Moses, "that you and your descendants may live . . . " Nor is this a one-time choice of some nebulous good; as the passage just before this in Deuteronomy points out clearly, the choices God offers us are not hidden in heaven, or across the seas, but are always near to us, in our hearts and on our lips.

What are the choices set before us today? Pope Francis quoted the bishops of Brazil in his apostolic exhortation *Evangelii Gaudium*: Take up daily the joys and hopes of all, but most particularly of those living on the margins and those who lack for the necessities of life. Those who have an abundance should tune their ears and consider the poor as "one with ourselves." This is the choice set before me, not my life or death, but to choose to notice and respond to the difficulties of those around me who are hungry and homeless, fleeing war or natural disasters.

What life do I choose today, for me, but above all for the poor?

Meditation: Consider what daily habits you have, or might develop, that keep you attentive to all God's people. What choices might you make today to bring life to those who you are aware are hungry, in need of shelter or care?

Prayer: With your Word on our lips and in our hearts, O Lord, help us to choose life in abundance: for ourselves, for our families, and for all the people of God.

Battle to Keep the Fast

Readings: Isa 58:1-9a; Matt 9:14-15

Scripture:
"This, rather, is the fasting that I wish:
   releasing those bound unjustly,
   untying the thongs of the yoke; . . .
Sharing your bread with the hungry . . . " (Isa 58:6-7)

Reflection: As I approach the age where I am no longer bound to the Lenten fast, I have to admit to a sense of relief. For most of my life, the prescribed fast was not a struggle, but over the last few years I have found the discipline an increasing challenge. I'm tempted to keep only to the letter of the law—leading to midnight raids on the refrigerator. I'm irritable and, frankly, by the end of the day, irritating as well, as I descend into the mire Isaiah describes: "quarreling and fighting, / striking with wicked claw." It's become all about me, a battle to keep the fast, a brawl with my own temper.

Certainly wrestling with hunger sharpens my sense of the experiences of those whose hunger gnaws at them day and night, and—I surely hope—softens my heart, and gives me eyes to see what hunger looks like where I live. And make no mistake about it, I am a sinner, and in need of penance.

But this unsparing reading from Isaiah is demanding that I step entirely outside of myself, putting aside my own penitence or my own desires to grasp the experience of hunger. Move, cries Isaiah, be at work, become the light in the darkness. Am I suffering in artificial solidarity with the hungry, for in truth I have enough to eat and more? Or am I going hungry because I have shared what I have with those who are hungry? Struggle not with your own hunger, not with your own needs, but fight for the needs of the hungry people in your cities and neighborhoods. This is the fast God requires of us.

Meditation: What is the fasting God desires of you this Lent? What particular skills do you have in abundance that you can use to actively assist those on the margins of your community?

Prayer: God of mercy and compassion, grant us generous hearts, that we might share freely with our brothers and sisters what we have in abundance. May the light of your glory be our guide.

An Invitation to Healing

Readings: Isa 58:9b-14; Luke 5:27-32

Scripture:
"I have not come to call the righteous to repentance but
sinners." (Luke 5:32)

Reflection: These first four days of Lent feel like a waiting
room, a space to pause before we plunge into wall-to-wall
Lent. A time to consider what I am to be about in this particular season. What is it that I most desire from God in this
time? Who is God calling me to become?

At the start of an interview with Pope Francis shortly after
he was elected, Fr. Antonio Spadaro, SJ, set aside his prepared questions and asked the pope, "Who is Jorge Mario
Bergoglio?" There was a long silence, after which Pope Francis responded, "I am a sinner." He went on to say, "I am a
sinner whom the Lord has looked upon," echoing a line from
a homily on the call of St. Matthew by the eighth-century
English monk Bede.

Listening to Luke's account of Jesus calling Levi in today's
gospel, I recall Pope Francis's response, "I am a sinner." I,
too, am a sinner. And because of that, the Lord has looked
upon me with love and compassion. Despite all the things I
have done, and have failed to do, all the times I have missed
the mark, I am called to sit down with Jesus. Now. This is

not a reward for the perfect, for the sinless, but an invitation to be healed.

What is it that I desire from God, now, this Lent? Healing, certainly, but also God's intimate companionship. Who is God calling me to become? Someone who eats and drinks with him, who follows closely in his footsteps as he walks among us.

Meditation: What is it that you desire from Lent? What are one or two areas where you seek Jesus' healing? What shape might that healing take? What habits might you put in place to splint the areas until they are fully healed?

Prayer: O Lord, we desire nothing more than to be close to you. Help us to hear you when you call. Grant us the grace to know your presence in our daily life, and the strength and courage to follow you wherever you go.

The Kingdom Breaks Through

Readings: Gen 9:8-15; 1 Pet 3:18-22; Mark 1:12-15

Scripture:
   "This is the time of fulfillment.
The kingdom of God is at hand.
Repent, and believe in the gospel." (Mark 1:15)

Reflection: The images in today's readings are arresting—devastating floods and burning deserts replete with wild beasts. And out of it all Mark shows us in today's gospel Jesus striding forth, proclaiming, Reform your lives! Believe in the Good News! The readings speak of pledges and covenants, of new life and a new kingdom. "This is the time of fulfillment. / The kingdom of God is at hand," cries Jesus.

   Today I hear Lent's clarion call: reform your life; today I find strength in Jesus' bold proclamation—the time has come, the kingdom of God is upon us. But will I go to my office tomorrow, without once thinking what might come to pass? The reign of God is at hand, surely, but come morning I'm likely to be caught up in a flood of papers to be marked and the roaring needs of cranky colleagues and desperate students.

   The Rev. Fred Rogers, who hosted the gentle TV show for children, *Mister Rogers' Neighborhood*, advised parents trying to explain frightening events to their children to "look for the helpers," that in times of trouble, someone always finds the strength to help. As Lent begins in earnest Jesus reminds me to cling to the Good News to believe that the kingdom of God is breaking through, even in my office, and to look around for the signs.

There are signs of the kingdom everywhere. The cross atop the church, stark against the sky, like a bow set in the clouds. God is here. The helpers, those who willingly walk into deserts and brave roiling waters, and those who tidy my classroom each morning so that I might teach and my students can learn.

The kingdom of God is within reach, Jesus tells us. Believe in the Good News, and be on the watch for the signs of the reign of God breaking through.

Meditation: Where do you see the reign of God breaking into your life? Look for the signs God has scattered through your daily life that point to the kingdom being at hand.

Prayer: Teach us to see the signs of the kingdom breaking through, O Lord. Show us those who work humbly to clear the path for you. Show us those who work for justice. Show us how to walk in your ways.

Be Holy

Readings: Lev 19:1-2, 11-18; Matt 25:31-46

Scripture:
"Be holy, for I, the LORD, your God, am holy." (Lev 19:2b)

Reflection: On one level these readings feel overwhelming, even terrifying. The first brims with "shall nots," while the gospel has Jesus threatening everlasting fire. All demand that I face what I have done and what I have failed to do, and the consequences of badly missing the mark. Fear the Lord, your God. But I begin to suspect that these readings are delving deeper, beyond how and when I've sinned, asking questions about identity and relationship. Mine and God's.

"But who do you say that I am?" (NABRE) Jesus asks Peter in a scene earlier in Matthew's gospel. In this gospel section we, too, are asked, "Who do you say that I am?" Who is God? "I am the LORD." This line punctuates Leviticus's less familiar listing of the ten commandments, pointing out to us God above. God is the reigning sovereign, God is the law giver. "[When] did we see you hungry or thirsty / . . . or in prison?" wonder the disciples. Jesus points to God with us, playing in innumerable places, in the words of priest and poet Gerard Manley Hopkins, SJ, each one's face a door into the holy, each one an opportunity to declare Jesus' identity.

Who do I say that Jesus is? I could, and do, echo Peter: "You are the Messiah, the Son of the living God" (NABRE). But it is not enough to know the answer; the answer cries out to be lived.

In both the "shalls" and "shall nots," we are being called to act as God acts. Choosing life, justice, and mercy. Who is God? The Holy One of Israel. Who am I made to be? The image and likeness of God. Fear the Lord; love your neighbor not only as yourself but as God incarnate. Be holy, as God is holy.

Meditation: Who do you say God is? In whose faces is it most difficult for you to see Christ? Where, today, can you choose to act as God would, tendering mercy and love?

Prayer: Your words, O Lord, are spirit and truth. Enlighten us, that we might see your truth clearly, that we might see your face in the faces of those we find difficult or troublesome. Strengthen us, that we might be justice for those oppressed and instruments of mercy to those in travail.

Radiant Mercy

Readings: Isa 55:10-11; Matt 6:7-15

Scripture:
Look to him that you may be radiant with joy . . .
   (Ps 34:6a)

Reflection: Joy seems to be Easter's territory, far off in these early days of Lent. But this line from the psalm resounds in my heart: "Look to [God] that you may be radiant with joy . . . " I hear in my head Marty Haugen's musical setting where this verse explodes right out of the refrain, without even a breath, as if we cannot contain ourselves, as if deep inside ourselves we understand how we were created to be: radiant with joy, our faces free from shame.

   Can I crack open the door to joy, even in the midst of Lent's privations? Perhaps if I knew what keeps my back at the door, holding it shut. The grievances to which I cling, the anger I stoke. Heaven forbid that my ability to forgive is the stick against which I will be measured. Or perhaps it's all that stuff that I hoard, just in case, until I'm consumed with worry about how to care for it all.

   Look to God when you pray, says Jesus, when the disciples asked for a lesson on prayer. Pray to look up so that our faces might be warmed in the light of God's love, that we might know where our joy lies. Pray to be opened to the joy that comes with letting go of our grasp on so many things. Be content with having today's needs met. Forgive others. Forgive ourselves. Forgive.

We don't need many words, just the Word that goes forth from God, bringing mercy, life, and joy to us, and will not return until it has achieved the end for which it was sent: That we might be radiant with joy, our faces free from all shame.

Meditation: The nineteenth-century French Catholic novelist Léon Bloy called joy "the most infallible sign of the presence of God." Where is joy erupting in your life, even in this Lenten desert? What does it tell you about God's will for you?

Prayer:
Our Father in heaven,
   hallowed be your name,
   your kingdom come,
your will be done,
   on earth as in heaven.
Give us today our daily bread;
and forgive us our debts,
   as we forgive our debtors;
and do not subject us to the final test,
   but deliver us from the evil one.

Beloved Sinners

Readings: Jonah 3:1-10; Luke 11:29-32

Scripture:
Have mercy on me, O God, in your goodness;
in the greatness of your compassion wipe out my
offense. (Ps 51:3)

Reflection: I have prayed Psalm 51 more than a thousand times, every Friday for more than thirty years. These days the Augustinian friars who staff my parish, and others of us who can, gather in the sun-drenched back chapel each morning for Lauds. Today I'm struck by the pastor's soft basso profundo from across the chapel, reciting the opening lines to this psalm: "Have mercy on me, O God, . . . wipe out my offense." I am momentarily taken aback to hear this man, whom I deeply respect for his integrity and faith, beg God for forgiveness. Aloud and in public. I am overset by the humility made manifest in this simple act, steadfastly repeated week after week, year after year.

Yet for all it asks us to face—our sinful natures, the times we have turned our faces away from God—there is incredible tenderness in this psalm. I am reminded of my mother, wiping my younger brothers' faces as they sat in the high chair, picking them up when they were done eating, and setting them firmly on their feet. All the while knowing that she will do this for them again and again, with calm good humor, until they learn to do such things for themselves.

Yes, we sin. Indeed, we are sinners. We long to turn toward God, but know we cannot do this by ourselves. But this psalm reminds us that even in our messy sinfulness, we are loved, not rejected or mocked. God stands by us, ever ready to renew us, to set us upright, once again grounded and balanced and ready to try our feet.

Meditation: Where do you see the greatest need for God's compassion and healing in your own life? Imagine standing in front of God, asking for his mercy. Pray the first lines of Psalm 51. How do you think God is responding to you, here and now?

Prayer: God of compassion, Son of justice, steadfast and holy Spirit, have mercy on us, for we are sinners. Cleanse us from all our faults and fashion for us humble hearts. Renew us in your love, make firm our steps, that we might ever walk in your ways.

A Shepherd's Care

Readings: 1 Pet 5:1-4; Matt 16:13-19

Scripture:
Tend the flock of God in your midst,
    overseeing not by constraint but willingly . . .
        (1 Pet 5:2)

Reflection: "They usually give birth at night, and the coyotes may try for the lambs," my dad said as he stowed an enormous flashlight next to my bed. He was entrusting me with his flock of two dozen sheep, seventeen of which were due to deliver in the next few days. I nearly turned around and went home. I was not equipped for this.

I worried the entire time he was away. How would I know if a ewe was in labor? Would I hear the coyotes in time to chase them off? The experience gave me a new, and frankly disconcerting, perspective on the oft-invoked images of shepherds in Scripture. My notion of shepherd had leaned toward the eighteenth-century romantic landscape painting, a canvas dotted with fluffy white sheep across a green sunlit meadow. The reality was me in pajamas and barn boots shouting at the coyotes in a dusty pasture at two a.m. trying to round up uncooperative ewes and their newborn lambs.

Eventually I learned to hear the rustlings as a ewe stamped her feet late in labor, to see the signs of a dangerously dehydrated lamb, and to lead the little ones into safety each evening, though the ewes never did take to me. I was still woefully unprepared, but I showed up nonetheless.

Before my stint as a shepherd, I thought these readings were not meant for me. I'm not the shepherd Peter has in mind in the first reading; neither were the keys to heaven entrusted to me, but rather to Peter and his successors in his chair. But now when I hear these readings I realize that we are all called to be shepherds. Even when we feel ill-equipped for the role, we are called to roll up our sleeves, grab our flashlights, and head out into the dust to look out for the flocks entrusted to us—our families, friends, colleagues, students. To keep our ears open to what is being born all around us.

Meditation: God's flock is in your midst, says Peter in the first reading. Where is the flock that has been entrusted to you? What might they need today to flourish? In what ways do you feel unprepared to care for them? Ask God to make you a better shepherd.

Prayer: Shepherd us, O God, and guide us in your paths. Grant us wisdom and courage, compassion and strength, so that we might faithfully tend those you have entrusted to our care. Guard your church, built of living stones, on the foundations you set.

Longing for Justice

Readings: Ezek 18:21-28; Matt 5:20-26

Scripture:
My soul waits for the LORD
  more than sentinels wait for the dawn. (Ps 130:6a)

Reflection: The psalmist longs for the Lord as long ago night watchmen would have longed for dawn, when they could stop worrying about what might be hiding in the darkness and take their rest. Still, I associate longing with Advent, not Lent. It's one thing to long for the infant Christ, wrapped warmly in images of angels singing "Joy to the world!" and wise kings bringing gifts, but quite another to long for Christ on the throne of judgment, calling me to account, laying bare my sins. Who could endure such scrutiny? Not me.

But this is precisely what I long for, in my depths: God's merciful eyes on me, searching for the virtues I have practiced, those things the prophet Ezra promised would wipe out my sins. I confess I would rather not worry about what I've hidden in the darkness, what might at any moment snatch me back into the depths. God cries out in joy when I call out, offering the gifts of mercy and forgiveness. Angelic choruses pale by comparison.

It's early yet in Lent, but today's psalm encourages us to yearn for an encounter with the God of justice. It promises us that this watchful longing will not be our lot forever. We are heard in our pleas for mercy. Forgiveness can be ours, in the measure that we use for others, and beyond. Lose no time, says Jesus in the gospel; practice mercy toward each other. Not just so we can avoid the fires of Gehenna, but so we might know firsthand what we thirst for. So we might know the profound joy it brings both to the one forgiven and to the One forgiving.

Meditation: Consider where God is calling you to experience the joy of mercy: Who can you forgive today? What do you need God to forgive you for? What virtues does God see in you?

Prayer: Compassionate God, Son of justice, in the depths of our hearts we desire to experience your healing mercy. Give us the strength to practice virtue, the courage to forgive those who have hurt us, and the humility to seek the forgiveness of those we have wronged.

February 24: Saturday of the First Week of Lent

To Reverence the Troublesome

Readings: Deut 26:16-19; Matt 5:43-48

Scripture:
"So be perfect, just as your heavenly Father is perfect."
  (Matt 5:48)

Reflection: I don't think I have any real enemies, anyone so hostile they are actively seeking my downfall. It's not that I think I'm so easy to get along with; I just suspect I'm not that important. Nor am I hatching any plots to ruin colleagues or neighbors. This in no way makes me perfect. Like poet and dramatist W. S. Gilbert, I have a little list of annoying people whose emails I might not miss. And yet I am still called to love them, to pray for their well-being, to receive them as Christ would.

Once every few weeks, the intercessions at Morning Prayer in the church's Liturgy of the Hours asks for forgiveness for the times when we've failed to see and reverence Christ in "the troublesome." Every time I squirm. That student who always comes late, the neighbor whose car alarm explodes the silence of my study with alarming regularity. These are the people I have a hard time loving. Perhaps I can pray for them, but love them? Reverence Christ in their persons? I wonder if I'd have an easier time if they were truly enemies.

Still, I find this call to be perfect as God is perfect to be as consoling as it is challenging. For if loving those who will not or cannot love you is what God does, then even when I fail to manage what God desires and cherish the troublesome and forgive the annoying, I am loved. Just as the sun rises and the rain falls inexorably on the just and the unjust, God loves the unloving as well as the loving. Even in my struggles to walk in God's ways, I am not forsaken.

Meditation: Madeleine L'Engle once suggested it was salutary to bless six people you didn't like before breakfast every day. Consider how you might bless one of the troublesome persons in your life today, either in prayer or in action.

Prayer: Teach us, O Lord, how to love as you love, without reservation, with all our heart and with all our soul. Grant us the grace to greet you with joy in all those we meet, particularly in the distressing and troublesome.

Saints and Prophets

Readings: Gen 22:1-2, 9a, 10-13, 15-18; Rom 8:31b-34; Mark 9:2-10

Scripture:
My vows to the LORD I will pay
 in the presence of all his people . . . (Ps 116:18)

Reflection: I have two beloved sons and no matter how many times I read the story of Isaac and Abraham in Genesis, I simply can't imagine myself walking in Abraham's shoes. I get entangled in the fear that must have consumed Isaac, and the grief that must have engulfed his father's heart, unable to grasp the depth of faith that propelled Abraham to this mountaintop. How could he?

And yet I brought both those sons to the font of my parish church at a Sunday Mass and pledged to give them over to God. My vows to the Lord, paid in the presence of the parish community. We clothed them in white garments, outward signs that they were now clothed in Christ. They were now bound as much to the mystery of Christ crucified as they were to Christ transfigured, his garments dazzling white. How could I?

Like Peter at the top of the mountain, I hardly know what to say. I say I believe, that I would sacrifice everything. I suspect that what I believe is that nothing so difficult would ever be demanded of me. I suspect what I really want is to stay safely atop the mountain, where everyone I see is clearly radiant. Saints and prophets. And make no mistake about this one, says God; this is my beloved son.

Down below amid the murky ordinariness of my life, I can't so easily tell the saints and prophets from the sinners and charlatans and no voices firmly point out where to find Jesus. Don't look, says the gospel, but listen. Don't get stuck on the visions of heaven, says Jesus; come down the mountain with me and let me show you how to become a saint and a prophet.

Meditation: Imagine Jesus showing up at your door and coming in for a cup of coffee. What would you say to each other? How long might he stay and what would you do when he left?

Prayer: God, give us the strength to follow your son's voice down from the mountaintop and out into the world. Grant that one day we might join with the saints and prophets, radiant in the joy of your love.

The Measure of a Gift

Readings: Dan 9:4b-10; Luke 6:36-38

Scripture:
"[G]ifts will be given to you;
  a good measure, packed together, shaken down, and
    overflowing,
  will be poured into your lap." (Luke 6:38a)

Reflection: In the fourth and fifth centuries, men and women fled to the Egyptian desert, seeking God in the silence and isolation of the bleak landscape. The wisdom of these desert solitaries was so renowned that people journeyed for months to ask them for a word of advice.

One of the desert fathers told a story of a monk living at Oxyrrynchos, charged with giving food to the hungry who came to the monastery's gates. A widow came, and the monk invited her to help herself to some barley. Before she left, he weighed her bag and scolded her for taking too much. After the embarrassed woman left, one of the other brothers asked the monk if the grain was a loan or a gift. The monk replied that it was a gift. "If you have given it to her as charity," asked the brother, "why did you quibble about the amount and put her to shame?"

Often, as I add a few things to my grocery cart for the local food pantry, or stock the cabinets at the parish's shelter for families in need of housing, I hear the question of this long-dead monk of Oxyrrynchos, "Is it a loan or a gift?" and reach for the good coffee and the diapers with the tapes that really stick. But as I listen to these readings again, I wonder about the less literal ways in which I weigh what I have to give to the last grain: the mental timer counting down in my head when I'm listening to the lonely neighbor I've run into at the gym; the head-down, I-didn't-see-you dash from my office to the copier; the slights I can't seem to forgive.

Is my life a loan to me or a gift for others? And if a gift, why am I quibbling over how much I'm giving?

Meditation: What do you keep stored up that you could share with those in need? What measure do you use with others—God's generous measure, or a scant cup? Do something small, but lavish, for someone else today. Consider letting someone in line ahead of you in traffic or at the grocery store.

Prayer: God, our very life is your gift. May we not count every grain, but pour out this gift without reservation on those in need of compassion and mercy, on those in need of food and shelter, on those who yearn for companionship.

A Bold Faith

Readings: Isa 1:10, 16-20; Matt 23:1-12

Scripture:
"[T]hey preach but they do not practice." (Matt 23:3b)

Reflection: Jesus chides the Pharisees in today's gospel for preaching good works while not practicing them. As a teacher and a parent, I try hard to practice what I preach. I carefully list the definition of every variable when working a quantum mechanics problem at the blackboard, no matter how tedious it seems. I clear my plate and "one common item" from the table at the end of a meal. My deeds are "drawn up before their eyes," to paraphrase the psalmist, as my kids strive to imitate how I balance a glass on my plate or my students reduce a complex equation to its roots.

I prefer an older, starker translation of this verse in Matthew—"Their words are bold but their deeds are few"—in part because I fear my words are often bold but, like my students grappling with messy problems, I have a tough time getting to the roots, to what I should be doing.

The former archbishop of Canterbury, Rowan Williams, writing of how our spiritual lives must extend beyond the theoretical and theological into our gritty day-to-day realities, says, "The greatness of the great Christian saints lies in their readiness to be questioned, judged, stripped naked and left speechless by that which lies at the center of their faith."

The center of my faith is Christ crucified. Jesus, who asks us not to lay burdens on each other's shoulders as the Pharisees did, but to pick up the cross, and follow him out into the world. The Word made flesh, speechless, yet not silenced. The bold Word has been spoken, on that cross at Calvary; what is required of me now is only to live that bold deed.

Meditation: What bold words have you spoken that you have failed to follow through on? What expectations do you have of others that you should be taking on yourself? Who do you consider as great saints, not for what they have said, but for what they have done?

Prayer: Jesus, show us how to be humble, to speak not with our mouths, but with our hands, with our whole selves. Grant us the strength to carry the crosses we see our neighbors struggling to bear, and the courage to boldly follow you wherever you go.

Unbound Grace

Readings: Jer 18:18-20; Matt 20:17-28

Scripture:
I hear the whispers of the crowd, that frighten me from
    every side,
  "as they consult together against me, plotting to take my
    life." (Ps 31:14)

Reflection: Could I drink of the cup that Jesus is offering to
Zebedee's sons James and John? Today's readings drove me
to dig out my tattered copy of the beautiful essay "On the
Experience of Grace" by Karl Rahner, SJ. In it, Rahner speaks
of the chalice that is offered to each of us, the wine within
tasting of Christ's sacrifice, his emptying out. We might not
always be able to drink from this cup, Rahner says; perhaps
the best we can do at a given moment is not to push the cup
away, but watch and wait. Trust in God's slow work.

I am moved by Rahner's tacit assumption that we all have
had moments when we have drunk from the chalice of grace.
We might, he says, occasionally sift through our own experiences. Look for the moments when we've said yes to renun-
ciation, yes to rising in the face of death and destruction, yes
to pouring ourselves out. For the times when some impulse
beyond ourselves has driven us to sacrifice, or when sacrifice
has brought us no sense of achievement, no pride. We ought

to search not so we know how far we've come in our spiritual journey, but that we might grasp how far we have to go.

I've read Rahner's essay so often it has become detached from the book. As I go to shelve it, pages of grace drift to the floor. Notice, it seems to say, the lived experience of grace. Detached. Scattered. Pulled from what has kept it bound, so that others might read it: in our faces and in our actions.

Meditation: Take a few minutes to gently search your own experiences. Can you see times when God was offering you to drink of the same cup as Jesus? Were there times when the cup being offered to you seemed particularly hard to drink? Consider asking God for the grace to hold those difficult chalices.

Prayer: Merciful Father, let your will be done in us this day. Grant us the humility to pour ourselves out for you, that we might experience a taste of the saving grace you have given the world in your son, Jesus Christ.

Take and Read

Readings: Jer 17:5-10; Luke 16:19-31

Scripture:
"They have Moses and the prophets.
Let them listen to them." (Luke 16:29b)

Reflection: The images the prophet Jeremiah uses are harsh: bushes that bear no fruit, lava wastes, fields sown with salt. They feel all the more so to me after hiking through lava fields last fall—blackened, fissured swaths of land scoured clean of life winding through lush grasslands. With no soil to hold the rocky surface in place, the gravel rolled under my feet, leaving me off balance, unstable, at risk. The ground had been cooling since before I was born, yet I still burned myself on steam roiling in a crack. Sulfurous mist swirled around the crater, eating away at skin and lungs. I longed to dive into a pool of cool water.

I have tasted salt and ashes in my life, too, stumbling when I encounter uncertain ground, looking for life and breath in places where there was none. I have committed sins that created seemingly uncrossable fissures between me and those I love. Between me and God.

Like the rich man in the gospel, who begged Abraham for a drop of water from Lazarus's hand, I long for the cool sweetness of consolation. Just a drop of holy water from a saint's hand and all will be well, I think. But as a single torrential rainstorm will not bring life back to the lava waste, neither is one drop enough to restore my soul, even from the hand of a saint.

Tolle lege, a voice called to St. Augustine in the garden one afternoon: take and read. "[You] have Moses and the prophets," I hear Abraham say. Meditate on God's law day and night, urges the psalmist. Let these streams of running water wear away the roughness of your stony heart. Root yourself deeply in the rich soil of the prophets. The readings encourage me to pick up the Scriptures: Take and read! Read to go beyond what is presented to me at Mass, and read to actively seek out the Word. Find ways to let Scripture's cool comfort wash over me day and night.

Meditation: What words of Scripture have you committed to memory, perhaps without even intending to? Consider how, over time, those words have changed your heart, your behavior. What words might you need to meditate on now, to slowly wear away the roughness in your soul?

Prayer: God of Abraham and Moses, whisper your words in our ears day and night, refreshing our souls, easing our hearts, making clear the way in which we should walk.

Dreaming with God

Readings: Gen 37:3-4, 12-13a, 17b-28a; Matt 21:33-43, 45-46

Scripture:
When his brothers saw that their father loved him best of
    all his sons,
      they hated him so much that they would not even greet
        him. (Gen 37:4)

Reflection: As one of a large, talkative family, I wonder what
it felt like for Joseph to be so isolated from all his brothers,
who had not a kind word for him, or perhaps any words at
all. And yet when his father asked, Joseph went the full distance and more to check on the well-being of a group of men
who wouldn't give him the time of day.

My ear is usually caught in this reading by the mention
of the twenty pieces of silver, the betrayal that prefigures
Judas and Christ. I wonder if subconsciously I'm eager to
get to Easter, to fast-forward to the story where I know there
is a happy ending. Yet the brothers' betrayal didn't start
with throwing Joseph into the cistern; it began when the
brothers—all of them—stopped saying hello to Joseph.

I suspect that like the brothers, there are more than a few
moments every day where I haven't a word for God. Praying
first thing in the morning? "Are we out of milk?" calls my
husband from the shower. At midday? There's a desperate

student knocking on my door. Surely I can find a moment at the end of the day? "Forgot, I have a meeting tonight, can you start dinner now?"

I don't set out to push God out of my daily life; it's a gradual thing. It's not malicious, but merely the clamor of the ordinary. Joseph's story reminds me that even when the urgent, and not-so-urgent, daily demands lead me to push off my time with God, God still finds his way in. Perhaps Joseph is not the only one whose dreams are God-sent.

Meditation: When do you fail to have a word for God in your daily life? Is it times when you are busy, or exhausted, or perhaps even angry or jealous? How does God find you? If not in your dreams, is there a quiet moment here or there in which God is inviting you to catch up with him?

Prayer: Lord, you are our beginning and our end. Help us to notice the moments in which you are inviting us to greet you, to hear the sustaining words you have for us, no matter how rushed or exhausted we are.

Bright Mercy

Readings: Mic 7:14-15, 18-20; Luke 15:1-3, 11-32

Scripture:
Who is there like you, the God . . .
Who does not persist in anger forever,
    but delights rather in clemency . . . ? (Mic 7:18)

Reflection: The first reading from Micah reminds us that God's mercy isn't grudgingly given, offered with a disappointed sigh. Nor is it meted out bit by bit, dispensed just in time, just enough. No, God *delights* in those moments when we return to him. It's hard for me to grasp.

When we are doing the forgiving, though it might bring us relief, it can be difficult to delight in it. Even when we have reconciled with those who have wronged us, bits of that disruption cling. We trust a bit less, or wince when a topic comes up. Yet in the gospel, we hear, "your brother was dead and has come to life again . . . " Wrap him in silks, bring on a feast. No chastising lectures, no veiled comments wondering how long he'll stay this time. Rejoice!

I once had a glimpse of that sort of joy, a tiny taste of what God might experience when we turn our faces back toward him. I was stuck in California on 9/11, unsure of when or how I would be able to return home and unwilling to promise a firm date to my five-year-old. When I finally came home, pulling into the driveway on a beautiful fall morning, Chris came bursting out the kitchen door, his face alight, crying, "You're alive!" He didn't quite realize that you couldn't talk to people in heaven on the phone, and he thought all the planes in the country had been destroyed, and everyone on them had died. His joy was overwhelming.

From time to time, I recall the brightness of joy I caught on Chris's face and wonder if that's how God will greet me when I return at last to his embrace. For now, I try to taste God's joy in my little resurrections, imagining his face radiant at each of my risings.

Meditation: Recall a time when you freely forgave someone who had abandoned you, even if it was just with the dirty dishes from dinner. What did it feel like? Was there a touch of joy in being able to give that kind of gift?

Prayer: Lord, pour out your mercy on each of our dyings: on our jealousies, on our grudges, on our failures to love, on all our sins. Grant us a glimpse of your joy in our healing.

Love's Odds

Readings: Exod 20:1-17 or 20:1-3, 7-8, 12-17; 1 Cor 1:22-25; John 2:13-25

Scripture:
"For I, the LORD, your God, . . .
   bestowing mercy down to the thousandth generation
   on the children of those who love me and keep my com-
      mandments." (Exod 20:5a, 6)

Reflection: God is a wrathful and jealous God. Or so this excerpt from Exodus seems to suggest, promising punishment on those who sin and their children, grandchildren, and great-grandchildren as well. But I'm married to a mathematician, and the mother of one as well, and know these questions about exponentially expanding sets—like descendants—are famously tricky, mathematical jests if you wish. The story is told of a woman who, having pleased the ruling emperor, was invited to name her reward. She asked for two grains of rice on the first day, and to have it doubled each day for a month. Though the reward seems small, four grains on the second day, eight on the third, only a teaspoon's worth total the first week, on the last day her reward was over a billion grains of rice.

My mathematical self tries to calculate if there are any circumstances under which God's wrath would actually be visited on the descendants of anyone who disobeyed him, given that God promises mercy to multiplying generations as well. Mercy is yours, says God in Exodus, if you have but one ancestor, somewhere in the previous thousand generations, who clung to God and obeyed these commandments. How long is a thousand generations? Twenty thousand years. Surely we all have at least one ancestor in that billion who loved God! The odds are in our favor.

This is our stumbling block, our folly, the idea that God's anger will spill over into the next generation, but the joke is on us; like the grains of rice in the mathematical folktale, God's mercy multiplies exponentially, outracing even his wrath. Love, he is telling us, always wins out.

Meditation: Who among your ancestors and relatives do you see as loving God in a particularly close way? How do you carry on their legacy of love? Imagine God saying to you, "You loved me so much, that I will shower mercy on you and all your kin, for the next twenty thousand years."

Prayer: God of our ancestors, Lord of our life, grant us the strength to cling faithfully to your laws. Let us not stumble, but recognize the saving power of Christ crucified, for all generations.

March 5: Monday of the Third Week of Lent

Ordinary Miracles

Readings: 2 Kgs 5:1-15b; Luke 4:24-30

Scripture:
> "[I]f the prophet told you to do something
> extraordinary,
> would you not have done it?" (2 Kgs 5:13b)

Reflection: A pan had boiled dry on the stove, leaving behind a sticky burnt mess. "Can you soak it in a special chemical?" wondered my husband, trusting I had something miraculous in my chemist's armamentarium. "I can," I assured him as I plunked the pot into a sink of hot water. He was skeptical, "Water?" Water is such an ordinary part of life, it's hard to imagine how extraordinary its properties are, at least to a chemist.

Naaman, too, thought he needed extraordinary means to cure him. All the resources he could command had not been enough to vanquish his leprosy. So he is dubious, and a bit miffed, when after he has mounted an elaborately equipped expedition to Israel, Elisha won't even see him, just sends him to wash in the local river. No ceremony, no prayers to the all-powerful God, no fancy vessels in which to carry the water. Go and wash. Trust me, says Elisha, this will work. Trust him, says the servant, what have you got to lose?

Like water, God is an ordinary part of our lives. All powerful, but also ever present. And as with water, we often find it hard to remember how truly extraordinary God's works are. We pray for miracles, but do we really trust we will be granted one? We are offered miracles, but can we recognize them when they come clad in the ordinary? Perhaps that is as it should be. I suspect it is God's way of being tender with us. Miracles are bubbling up everywhere he touches, but if we were to notice, we might be terrified of such power at work in our lives.

The pot came clean. Miraculously clean, said my husband. Trust me, says God, I can work miracles with the ordinary.

Meditation: In a blessing for those who are exhausted, poet and priest John O'Donohue suggested slowing down to notice the miracles you might have rushed through. When has God come to your rescue in ordinary ways? What miracles have you rushed through? When have you been a prophet for others, offering everyday help in need?

Prayer: All-powerful and ever-living God, give us the eyes to see the miraculous in the ordinary. Help us to trust in your help, even when we cannot see the way forward.

Saints from Ashes

Readings: Dan 3:25, 34-43; Matt 18:21-35

Scripture:
"Do not let us be put to shame,
    but deal with us in your kindness and great mercy."
        (Dan 3:41b-42a)

Reflection: I know the first reading by heart. It is the prayer of the three young men who have been thrown into the fiery furnace by the king of Babylon for refusing to worship alien gods, which appears regularly in the four-week cycle of canticles in the Liturgy of the Hours.

I wonder at these ancient saints, Azariah, Hananiah, and Mishael. And perhaps because I share a name with Mishael, I wonder whether I could ever be his sort of saint, calling on God at every opportunity, praying when my life is on fire, and I fear I might have been abandoned by God.

The gospel speaks of equally extravagant offerings. Forgive, says Jesus, again and again. Not just with words, but with my whole heart. Maybe I could be that sort of saint? Merciful and forgiving, even when I've been hurt over and over, ground into dust by disappointment.

I am poor saint material, I fear. Like Peter in the gospel, I want God to assure me that there are limits on what might be asked of me, that those bumper stickers that promise God won't give you more than you can handle are true. In truth, I suspect saints are pulled from the ashes of fires that are more than they can handle.

What I hear in these readings is that as much as I have limits, God has none. God is not put off by raging fires, or even by my failures to forgive. Perhaps this is the sort of saint I can be, one whose life has collapsed into the ash heap of sin, and who can do nothing but wait on God to pull me out. Like Azariah in the first reading, I cry, "Deliver [me] by your wonders, . . . O Lord."

Meditation: What in your life is more than you can handle? What has been crushed beyond recognition by your transgressions? Are you prepared to let God reach into the ashes of these experiences and rescue you? What kind of saint would you be?

Prayer: Remember us, O Lord! In your mercy, search for us when we're buried under the ashes of our sins, and when we stand in the raging fires of disaster we cannot handle. Deliver us by your wonders; restore our life.

Embattled with the Everyday

Readings: Deut 4:1, 5-9; Matt 5:17-19

Scripture:
"For what great nation is there
    that has gods so close to it as the Lord, our God, is to us
    whenever we call upon him?" (Deut 4:7)

Reflection: At this time of year, when the weather is chancy and damp in Philadelphia, I rejoice at the appearance of a feast on the church's calendar, even one of martyred mothers. The bright flash of red vestments rounding the corner out of the sacristy, after weeks of dull violet days, rouses me from the doldrums. It is the memorial of Perpetua and Felicity, two young mothers who died in the third century.

Perpetua's prison diaries are the earliest piece of Christian writing we have from a woman's hand and though we are separated by centuries and I'm unlikely to be thrown to wild beasts, her concerns seem not so different from mine. She, too, is stretched taut between generations, worried about her infant son and whether he is gaining weight and about her fraught relationship with her elderly father. Even her little troubles are familiar—as she hunts for a hairpin to put her hair back up after it gets disheveled in the arena.

God granted Perpetua extraordinary serenity during her imprisonment and martyrdom. She is said to have steadied the hand of the gladiator who was about to kill her. I'm tempted to think that such grace is given only to the legendary martyrs and saints, but the preface to Perpetua's diary notes that these experiences are being shared with the faithful precisely to dispel the idea that such things only happened long ago to the very holy. No, such signs are always appearing, God's power made visible not just for those who do not yet believe, but as a gift to those of us who already do. Even when the rack we have been stretched out upon is simply that of our everyday responsibilities, God's calming Spirit steadies us.

Meditation: Where am I so stretched by my responsibilities today that I need God to grant me calm and composure? Where do I feel embattled in my faith, and where do I struggle to be faithful to God?

Prayer: Most Holy Spirit, bring us comfort in our everyday difficulties; help us collect ourselves when we are stretched between demands. Dwell in us and dispel the gloom that clouds our hearts.

Spiritual Stretching

Readings: Jer 7:23-28; Luke 11:14-23

Scripture:
If today you hear his voice, harden not your hearts.
(Ps 95:7b, 8a)

Reflection: Hard hearts and stiff necks. Deaf ears and mute tongues. There is so much bodily imagery in today's readings. For me, our modern ability to see inside a living human body heightens its impact. A hardened heart is not a rhetorical device. I know what a stiff, calcified heart looks like; I've seen it unable to beat freely, unable to respond to the demands my father was placing on it, the life force literally turning to stone within him.

When we are ill or injured, we can feel as if our selves are divided. Our minds will send the command, "Bend over and tie your shoes," and our bodies respond, "You must be joking?" It's an uncomfortable feeling, and so we adjust our routine, often without realizing it, choosing shoes that slip on—just for today, we murmur; next week we'll sign up for that class at the gym.

I worry that I've gradually adjusted to having a spiritual stiff neck and hardened heart. That I've substituted slip-on prayers for the more demanding stretching that it would take to pray for those I find unlikable or troublesome. That

I'd rather remain on my knees in prayer than walk briskly into the world to be God's hands, to lift the crosses and chase away the darkness.

What would it take to stretch my stiff neck, until I can turn around and see what God is about in this time and place? What would it take to soften my heart until it is able to respond to the demands God places upon it? Listen to the psalmist: sing joyfully, bow down. Listen to the prophets: deal justly with your neighbor, welcome the immigrants, be the peacemaker.

Meditation: Just before today's selection from the prophet Jeremiah, God gives a prescription for healing Israel's stiff neck: deal justly with neighbors and strangers, be attentive to those on the margins of the community. In which of these areas are you least able to act? Do one thing to gently stretch toward God in this area.

Prayer: God, cast out from us all that divides us from you. Strengthen our hearts, and ease our stiff necks. Open our ears to hear your voice in the voices of the prophets, and free our tongues to praise you joyfully.

Unburdened

Readings: Hos 14:2-10; Mark 12:28-34

Scripture:
"Return, O Israel, to the LORD, your God;
   you have collapsed through your guilt." (Hos 14:2)

Reflection: Last summer, I spent three weeks working at the Vatican Observatory, in a picturesque village in the hills outside Rome. Early in the morning of my last day in Castel Gandolfo, I grabbed my now haphazardly packed bags, plopped them onto my luggage cart, and headed out, intending to walk the two miles down the hill to the lab. The same two miles I had walked with ease each day.

But as my cart rocked its way across the cobblestones, the bag on top kept slipping off, forcing me to stop again and again. I was ready to collapse from the weight of it all before I reached the end of the block. Not to mention, the sun that had warmed the balcony while I drank my tea had vanished behind a threatening cloud. I resigned myself to a tortuous, wet walk.

And then a colleague from the Observatory appeared, walking up the hill. "Can I give you a ride?" Fr. Paul offered. I suddenly could empathize with the psalmist whose shoulder has been relieved of the burden, whose hands were freed from the basket.

The experience pushed me to ruthlessly repack my bags before I flew home, leaving behind books already read and extra chocolate, tossing those extra napkins from the espresso bar. So, too, does Lent push me to dig out of my soul all the things that have clogged my heart, the little sins that I clench in my fists, keeping me from opening my hands freely. Now that I can see what I'm carrying, I wonder that I don't collapse from the guilt of it all. But today God is offering to not only lift the burden from my shoulders, but also to help in rebalancing my load in the future. Tossing those small habits, pushing aside bitterness and rancor, so that I might love God with my whole heart, and with all my strength.

Meditation: What is weighing you down? How might you prayerfully sort through what takes up room in your heart and mind? What can you let God carry for you? What habits and grudges can be cleared out, left behind?

Prayer: God of Israel, take away what clutters our hearts, feed us with your Word, so that we might have the strength and freedom to love you with all our hearts, all our souls, all our being.

Who Am I?

Readings: Hos 6:1-6; Luke 18:9-14

Scripture:
For it is love that I desire, not sacrifice,
    and knowledge of God rather than burnt offerings.
        (Hos 6:6)

Reflection: The Pharisee is quick to point out to God—and to anyone who is within earshot—what he is not. He is not dishonest, not greedy. He is equally quick to say the good he does; he tithes, he fasts. But the tax collector says only who he is: a sinner. And he does it not just with words, but with his whole being, bowing his head and beating his breast.

Who am I? I have an "About the Author" section on my website that says I'm a mother, a wife, a practicing Roman Catholic, a teacher, a lover of chocolate. It's there so that readers might have a sense of what experiences and perspectives I bring to my writing. I hope, too, that my readers and I might find something in common, whether it's teaching or the practice of a faith or a favorite food.

Who am I in this gospel? I am, alas at times, the Pharisee. I'm not immune to pointing out who I'm not or what good things I do. I am not like that black SUV, I say to my son in the car; I'm not the sort to run a stop sign. Until, of course, I am.

It would work just as well if my biography simply read: I am a sinner. It is what binds us together; we are all sinners, wherever we stand, however we pray. It is the only experience I can write from, that of a sinner, beloved by God. It would be better still if I could say this not just with my tongue, but with my whole being. Not that I might belittle myself, but that I might know in my depths how much I am loved by God. That I might grasp that even in my frailty, and with all my failings, God will tenderly wash it all away, desiring only that I grow to know him and love him more deeply.

Meditation: How would you describe yourself to God in one or two sentences? Now imagine how God might describe you in return. What is it that God finds delightful in you?

Prayer: Lord, we come before you as sinners, longing for mercy and forgiveness. Give us the eyes to see ourselves as you do, sinners beloved by God. Give us the eyes to see others as you do, beloved sons and daughters.

Refashioned

Readings: 2 Chr 36:14-16, 19-23; Eph 2:4-10; John 3:14-21

Scripture:
"But they mocked the messengers of God,
   despised his warnings, and scoffed at his prophets . . ."
      (2 Chr 36:16a)

Reflection: The first reading opens with Judah's fall, the survivors taken captive and sent to exile in Babylon, punished for scoffing at the prophets and mocking the messengers of God.

I don't want to face the questions this reading is raising in my heart. Have I mocked messengers from God, scoffed at the prophets, placed my desires ahead of God's? Surely I have, for we all have. Still, I want to race ahead to the ending, to the Israelites' release from captivity. I want to skip past the psalm with its poignant imagery of a people stripped even of their songs, to Paul's assurance to the Ephesians: God is rich in mercy, and by God's favor I am saved.

We have reached the midpoint of Lent, still walking through the ashen landscape of our sins, but quickening our pace toward the rich pools of mercy we see shimmering in the distance. We are a people in exile, who realize their release is at hand.

It's also Laetare Sunday, named for the first words of the traditional opening antiphon in Latin, *Laetare, Jerusalem!*, "Rejoice, Jerusalem!" I am tempted today to rejoice at having made it this far through Lent's desert, to look back at what I have accomplished, what I've managed to give up and to take up. But Lent is not a self-improvement program, nor is it a self-denial challenge, with badges to be earned for each day or week I manage not to eat chocolate. Lent is a time for us to be open to God's refashioning of us. Our salvation is not our own doing, it is not a reward, and we should not take pride in it, says St. Paul in the second reading.

The true cause for rejoicing is not whether I manage to keep to my Lenten practice of penance, but that *regardless* God sends forth his love and his mercy to rescue me. He will bring me back to the mountain where he dwells, to lift my face to God, who is my joy.

Meditation: Sundays are never days of penance in the Catholic tradition, even in Lent, but always joyful celebrations of our salvation. What has God rescued you from this week that gives you cause for joy? How has God begun to refashion you this Lent?

Prayer: You so loved your people, Lord, that you sent us your only begotten son to lead us out of our exile and into the joyful light of your kingdom. Continue to refashion our hearts, so that we might be drawn out of the darkness.

March 12: Monday of the Fourth Week of Lent

Unfailing Dawns

Readings: Isa 65:17-21; John 4:43-54

Scripture:
You changed my mourning into dancing . . . (Ps 30:12)

Reflection: "At nightfall, weeping enters in, / but with the dawn, rejoicing." These lines of Psalm 30 are set deep into my heart. In the dark hours of a Holy Thursday morning many years ago, I paced a surgical waiting room reciting this psalm. At nightfall, there had been weeping, as my young husband was rushed into surgery. Now the reports from the surgeon were increasingly dire. Our families were thousands of miles away. My rosary and my prayer book were in my purse, left behind as I ran to the ambulance. I had nothing to pray with but the scraps of the psalms. *Hear me, Lord, and rescue me.*

Over and over, I thought, no matter how much I weep tonight, there will be joy in this dawn. Tom will survive the surgery and I will rejoice. Or he will not, and instead wake to the joy of heaven. Though my tears flowed through the darkness that night and into Tom's funeral, I couldn't quite shake the sense of dawn, just beyond my reach.

When I remarried, in the brilliant light of a September day, we used this psalm in the liturgy. Drenched in joy, I could still taste the salt of those mourning tears, still sense the night waiting to creep in.

In all our lives, there will be mourning, there will be joy, often inextricably linked; we cannot mourn if we did not love. I think of earth rotating in space, so that at every moment somewhere on earth darkness is falling and somewhere dawn is unfailingly breaking. The light is always there flooding the solar system, waiting for the moment our side of the earth turns to face it. So, too, I trust that all my nights will end in a dawn, in the ever-present light of God's face.

Meditation: What prayers do you find yourself reaching for when you are troubled or in distress? Is there a particular snippet of Scripture you find consoling that you might commit to memory, or keep on a slip of paper in your purse or wallet?

Prayer: Write your words upon our hearts, Lord, that we might find them when we are in dire straits. Grant us the grace to know that your light will dawn upon us, no matter how dark the night seems.

Stirrings

Readings: Ezek 47:1-9, 12; John 5:1-16

Scripture:
When Jesus saw him lying there
> and knew that he had been ill for a long time, he said to
> > him,
"Do you want to be well?" (John 5:6)

Reflection: The stirrings tell me my class time is nearly up. Books close with a snap, pencil cases zip shut, while chairs slide back so their occupants can make a quick exit. "Thank you," I say at the end of each lecture, and chaos erupts. Some students dash out the door to their next class; others rush up to my desk at the front. "I'm confused," says one. "I'm behind on my homework," confesses another. In this scrum, help goes to the loudest, the fastest, the pushiest—not always the ones who need it most.

This is how I imagine the chaos of the pool at Bethesda, the sound as the waters stir, the rush to get down to the water, the hopes that are stirred up in the paralyzed, abandoned man, and then squelched as people push past. The weakest, the ones most in need of the healing waters, are left behind.

I wonder, who do I step on, push past, intent on becoming healed myself? I am reminded of one of St. John Chrysostom's homilies, often sharply summarized as, "If you cannot find Christ in the beggar at the church door, you will not find him in the chalice." Am I rushing past people who need help in my haste to tend to my own spiritual needs?

To be Christ is not just to bustle in to feed the hungry and clothe the poor; it is first of all to notice, to see, to approach, and to ask. Jesus notices the man by the side of the pool, sees what he might need, and asks him, "Do you want to be well?" Nor does Jesus heal and withdraw; with the healing came relationship. Jesus seeks the man out again.

Your brothers and sisters, said St. John Chrysostom, are "the most precious temple of all." Look out for them, draw near, and linger with them—so that the Body of Christ, entire, might be healed.

Meditation: What is keeping you from being forgiven your sins? What obstacles are you placing in the way of those around you who need healing in body or in soul? Who are you rushing past?

Prayer: Plunge us, O Lord, into your healing pool of grace. Stir up our souls so that we might see the troubled and those in pain around us. Give us the wisdom to know what our sisters and brothers need and the courage to bring it to them.

Patient Powers

Readings: Isa 49:8-15; John 5:17-30

Scripture:
I will cut a road through all my mountains,
 and make my highways level. (Isa 49:11)

Reflection: One October morning I took a boat out from a tiny Irish harbor to see the cliffs near Slieve League, which rise almost two thousand feet straight up out of the sea. The rock face has been shorn away, revealing deposits that once ran in neat horizontal layers now wrenched vertical, the layers of rock folded over and over upon each other, like a child playing with clay. I am astounded by the forces that could wrest this ancient bedrock, laid down five hundred million years ago, from the sea bed. I am awestruck by powers that could pleat and crease rock like paper, then pull off half a mountain to reveal what has been done.

God promises in the first reading to cut through mountains, to lay them level. I think of the cliffs at Slieve League, grasping anew the power lurking in Isaiah's imagery. These are not inconsequential forces at play; he says that he can fold rocks like dough, level the land, cut roads through mountains, rescue us. And like the rocks, folded by pressures applied over eons, I find myself grasping that God will be as patient and as tender with us, not crushing us into dust in an instant.

I imagine this power brought to bear on me, God's hands on me like a potter's. Wrenching up from my depths my faults, laid down over years, cutting through to the center, so that I might see the damage that fans out, and what must be done to make it level again. If I allow it, if I desire it, the forces that could shape cliff and mountaintop and valley can reshape my life. Gently but inexorably pushing and pulling at my stony heart.

Meditation: The forces that shaped the earth and the heavens are still at play. Look today for one of those signs, whether it is a bulb forcing itself through frozen ground or a tree pushing aside the sidewalk. Imagine God pulling you gently through a difficult ground, not only unharmed, but ready to flourish.

Prayer: The heavens and earth sing of your power to change us, God. Do not crush our spirit, but may your tender compassion soften our hearts of stone and smooth away the imperfections.

Demands at the Door

Readings: Exod 32:7-14; John 5:31-47

Scripture:
"[John] was a burning and shining lamp,
    and for a while you were content to rejoice in his light.
But I have testimony greater than John's." (John 5:35-36a)

Reflection: I'm never more distractible than when facing a stack of papers to mark. I know what needs to be done, I know that I have to do it, but suddenly the laundry begs to be folded and shouldn't I check my email—in case a student has questions, of course. Oh, look at that cute cat meme. Thirty minutes later I resurface, laundry folded, emails answered, and my knowledge of felines expanded. But the papers are still unmarked.

Like the Israelites in the desert and John's followers in the gospel, at times I find my eyes fixed on what's right in front of me, tending to the gods of the immediate. It's the moment when I check my phone out of boredom—or to be sure of my own importance—rather than take a breath of time with God, to whom I am important. It's the little flames of anger and jealousy sending up puffs of pride that I tend so carefully, instead of letting my prayers rise like incense.

It is even the good things and people in my life; when there are so many needs I am meeting, I have no time to consider what direction God desires I go in. All too soon I can't find God for all the demanding deities I've crammed onto my altar in this world.

How can I look away from these idols I've set up? In today's gospel, Jesus does not offer us "ten steps to a better, more focused you." Listen to Moses, he says, who begged for our lives, reminding God that we are his cherished people. Come to me, he says; I am the life you want to possess. Put me at the center and see the clamoring demands, both the critical and the trivial, through my eyes.

Meditation: Check your calendar or to-do list. What draws your gaze today? What fires are you tending? Ask yourself, how does God desire to love you—right now—in the midst of these everyday demands? How can you find time today to respond to that love?

Prayer: Remember us, God, even when we cannot seem to keep our eyes fixed on you. Give us the grace to see through the thicket of daily demands and know that we are loved at every moment. Grant us the courage to respond to your love and so to follow you ever more closely.

Unbounded Hope

Readings: Wis 2:1a, 12-22; John 7:1-2, 10, 25-30

Scripture:
"[M]erely to see him is a hardship for us,
Because his life is not like that of others,
   and different are his ways." (Wis 2:14b-15)

Reflection: In early February of 1945 Alfred Delp, SJ, a Jesuit priest and philosopher, was executed for resisting the Nazis. For months, his hands were bound by chains, because his guards feared what he might do. What he did was celebrate Mass, bound on earth, but not in heaven. I wonder what his guards thought. Did the sight of this man—so filled with faith he could joke with the prison chaplain as he walked to his execution, "In thirty minutes, I shall know more than you do"—trouble them at all?

   I surely brush past saints every day. Every once in a while, I actually crash into one, startled to look up and see a face alight with God. But I'm afraid to deliberately look for the blessed among us. It's hard enough to hear of the faith and courage of long-dead saints, but to see what it looks like here and now is more than I can bear. Their lives, ordinary lives, lives much like my own in many ways, show me what is possible in my own life.

Like the residents of Jerusalem, who couldn't imagine a Messiah whom they knew well, I'd rather think that the saints are not like me at all, their origins a mystery, their strength and courage drawn from fonts that I have no access to. I'd rather pretend that holy men and women are bound in books, where the whole story is laid out, the happy ending certain. I'd rather look the other way, lest I be thought mad or conceited.

Delp wrote that we should pray for clear vision, to see the holy ones among us, to hear what they proclaim. Pray for hope, which sees what the world and we who dwell in it can be. Pray that we can hope to be saints. "Is it madness to hope—or conceit, or cowardice, or grace?" Delp wondered. Madness, perhaps, but certainly not cowardice. And always and everywhere, hope in nothing but the grace of God.

Meditation: Who are the people in your life who are hopeful, perhaps even in the face of ridicule? What do their lives call you to be? Whose lives give you pause, rousing you from apathy?

Prayer: God, be near to us. Rouse us so that we might see the saints among us. Teach us by their lives how to be people of hope in our day, patient in times of trouble, steadfast in the face of evil.

Learning to Stand

Readings: Jer 11:18-20; John 7:40-53

Scripture:
"Look and see that no prophet arises from Galilee."
  (John 7:52b)

Reflection: "Know where you stand, and stand there," said priest and poet Daniel Berrigan, SJ—this was reportedly the entirety of his commencement address at Xavier High School in New York. Vengeance, violence, cries the first reading. We see an uneasy crowd, perched on the edge of violence in the gospel. Where do I stand in that scene, where Jesus is preaching, the crowd whispering, and the Pharisees hatching plots? Do I even know?

These readings turn my soul out onto the table, asking me where I stand, searching for the answer I might give to the Pharisees' question: "Why did you not bring him?" I want my answer to be that of the guards and of Nicodemus: Because I have heard him.

But here I stand, confronted by today's gospel, uncertain of my response. I recognize the awful ways we can whip a crowd, even a crowd of one—myself—into anger, winding wrongs around myself like barbed wire around a pasture until it is hard to hear myself, let alone Jesus. I see too how easy it is to cast doubts like so many stones: surely you haven't been taken in; look it up, the prophet will not come from Galilee!

The gospel today demands an answer, asks that we know where we stand. But how can I be sure of my ground? Before you decide, says Nicodemus in the gospel, the law asks that you stand there and listen. How else can you know who stands before you? Rumor? Hearsay? To discern, I must first listen, not to the crowd, but to God's voice within my heart. And so I pray to know where I stand, and I pray to be able to stand there.

Meditation: Where do you stand? Why? What have you heard that tells you this is the Messiah, the Christ?

Prayer: God, who searches our hearts and knows us in the depths of our being, open our ears so that we may hear your Word over the noise of the crowd; speak to our hearts so that we know where we must stand; strengthen our resolve so that we may stand there.

Free to Walk

Readings: Jer 31:31-34; Heb 5:7-9; John 12:20-33

Scripture:
I will place my law within them and write it upon their
hearts . . . (Jer 31:33b)

Reflection: After I fractured my foot falling down some icy
steps, I used crutches for several weeks. They were a pain.
It was hard to get in and out of the car, and they crashed
noisily to the floor if I didn't prop them carefully enough
against the wall. Worst of all they made it impossible to carry
a cup of tea from the kitchen to my favorite chair. I rejoiced
when the surgeon replaced the crutches with a boot that
cradled my foot, freed to move without having to think about
external supports.

In the first reading from Jeremiah, God promises Israel a
new covenant. Not one that burdens them, which must be
painstakingly learned, or dragged about on tablets, but one
that resides within them, readily available. A covenant that
will, as the psalmist sings, sustain in them a willing spirit,
give them again joy in their salvation. We believe that the
mediator of this new covenant of joy, now situated in the
core of our being, is Christ. With this law planted in our
hearts we are freed to walk. We become free to serve, because
we no longer have to hold ourselves up.

The bones in my foot are long mended, but I have not lost my sense of wonder at how my ankle bears my weight, the tiny twinge as I go down the stairs reminding me of the incredible healing that has taken place within me. How much more am I in awe of the healing God has wrought? I pray in the psalm that God might have mercy on me, that my offenses might serve to remind me of the enormity of God's mercy.

Meditation: What within you braces up your faith? Where might you need external support? Do you set aside time to seek God's law within your heart? What seeds is God bringing to life in you?

Prayer: God, in the secret recesses of our hearts, show us where you have planted your law, so that we might know what must be healed. Let your mercy wash over us, and buoy us up with your love, so that we might follow you faithfully throughout our lives.

Risking Love

Readings: 2 Sam 7:4-5a, 12-14a, 16; Rom 4:13, 16-18, 22; Matt 1:16, 18-21, 24a or Luke 2:41-51a

Scripture:
He is our father in the sight of God,
    in whom he believed, who gives life to the dead
    and calls into being what does not exist. (Rom 4:17)

Reflection: There is a statue of St. Joseph in the small chapel where I often go to Mass. He has Jesus comfortably on his hip, his face suffused with love for his child. Every time I see it, I think of my husband, our sons propped on his hip as he put away the dishes or wrote on the blackboard. My sons are men now and, in the way they walk and stand, the expressions they use, I see their father clearly.

Who is St. Joseph? The gospels say only he was an upright man. But looking at my own sons, I realize we see St. Joseph in the gospels again and again, every time we encounter Jesus, for surely we would see his adoptive father in him just as we see his heavenly Father. When Jesus stood in the synagogue and opened the scrolls to Isaiah to proclaim, "The Spirit of the Lord GOD is upon me" (NABRE), I see St. Joseph with his young son on his hip as he listened to the law and the prophets. Each time his son withdrew into the hills to be with God, I see St. Joseph striding up the road, a psalm on his lips.

Where is St. Joseph in the passion? We assume he must be dead, or perhaps too ill or elderly to travel, for surely he would have been at the cross with his son and his wife if he could. But I see him there, too. Some legends say St. Joseph was a widower, and Mary his second wife. As a widow who has remarried, I wonder if what St. Joseph the widower showed Jesus in his human capacity was how to stretch out your arms to embrace love, with the certain knowledge that to love is to risk great loss and suffering. And in doing so, perhaps Joseph shows us how to do the same.

Meditation: Who are the upright and holy people in your life who have shaped your relationship with God? What is the most important lesson you think you learned from them?

Prayer: Pray for us, St. Joseph, that we, too, might be upright and holy people, alert to the Word of God, ready and able to stretch out our arms in love no matter the cost.

Whom the World Cannot Hold

Readings: Num 21:4-9; John 8:21-30

Scripture:
"You belong to this world,
   but I do not belong to this world." (John 8:23b)

Reflection: I have a photograph on my computer desktop of a twelfth-century fresco of the harrowing of Hades. The original covers the dome of a small chapel of the Church of the Holy Savior in Istanbul. Jesus is pulling Adam and Eve up from the netherworld, his arms stretched across a lunette, his legs firmly planted. Their hands are still limp in his, their eyes just opening to see Christ's face above them. Ribbons of light unfurl beneath his feet, his power evident to the surrounding cloud of witnesses, the prophets, and the apostles—and to me. Each time the photo comes up I think, *this* is God from God; the world has no hold on him.

The world cannot hold me, says Jesus in today's gospel, for "I AM." His power comes from who he is: "I AM," the one, true God. We, meanwhile, are bound to this world, groaning in distress and mired in sin, praying to be released, powerless to save ourselves. We live, says Jesus, only because we believe.

I believe. I believe in God. I believe in his only begotten Son, and the Holy Spirit. But in my worst moments, when, like the Israelites in the desert, my patience is worn out and calamities are around every corner, I wonder if I truly believe that I will live. I am comforted by St. Augustine, who, in reflecting on this gospel, said believing in God is not first and foremost to believe in life eternal, or even in the resurrection. To believe in "I AM" is rather to abide in God, to let God hold you. This I certainly believe, that God has me by the hand, pulling me out of this life and into the next.

Meditation: What chafes at your life? What seems dull and without flavor? Do you need rescue, to be pulled out? Has your sense of gratitude failed you?

Prayer: Incline your ear to us, O God, for we are worn thin by distress. Bend down from heaven to pull us free from the things that bind us to this world.

Living Into Truth

Readings: Dan 3:14-20, 91-92, 95; John 8:31-42

Scripture:
"If you remain in my word, you will truly be my disciples, and you will know the truth, and the truth will set you free." (John 8:32)

Reflection: As a scientist, truth is something I'm willing to give up much for. I have spent sleepless nights running calculations on a supercomputer. I've stood at the stove, scrawling equations on the kitchen blackboard with one hand while stirring soup with the other. Each truth I uncover offers me a clearer understanding of the universe, a glimpse of God seen in the firmament of heaven and in the depths of the atom. It's a way of life, not just my job.

In the gospel, Jesus suggests we must similarly live our way into the truth of our faith, that if we order our lives as he teaches, if we dwell within the Word, we will know the truth. Belief is not just one piece of our lives; it is our life.

But while truth in science leads to a greater clarity about the created world, in a homily for the feast of St. Thomas Aquinas, theologian Karl Rahner, SJ, suggests that searching for the truth in the spiritual realms leads in precisely the opposite direction. The purpose, he says, of our struggles with the underpinnings of our faith is to force us away from clarity, deeper into the mystery that is God. It is not to grasp onto some fact, like a telephone pole in a gale force wind, but to let ourselves be moved. The end of our theological explorations should not be the mastery of a set of rules, but a willingness to allow ourselves to be overpowered by God.

This truth simultaneously binds us to Christ and sets us free to move, free to love God, infinite and unbounded, with inexhaustible joy.

Meditation: Today's responsorial psalm is a litany of praises for God, who is "exalted above all forever." God on his throne, God in the depths, God in the heavens. What truths about God bring you to joyfully praise him? Try praying them as a litany: "Blessed are you . . . praiseworthy and exalted above all forever."

Prayer: Blessed are you, God, who day by day calls us deeper into your mystery. Lead us toward the truth, teach us to live by your commands, until we return to you forever in joy.

Know Him as God

Readings: Gen 17:3-9; John 8:51-59

Scripture:
"Amen, amen, I say to you,
    before Abraham came to be, I AM." (John 8:58b)

Reflection: John's gospel is not for the faint of heart; between the mystical imagery and the carefully structured narrative, it can seem unapproachable and opaque. Yet of all the gospels, scholars tell us that John's is most deeply situated in the place and times Jesus lived. The scenes are set in known places; the descriptions of day-to-day life and prayer are precise. For me, the details, like the one in the gospel today where the crowd tells us that Jesus isn't anywhere near fifty years old, anchor the story to a world I know, while the imagery and language hint that the barrier between heaven and earth is thin, thinner than I might wish to imagine.

John does not care to leave an account of a transfiguration seen only by the apostles, or report the times Jesus cautioned those he healed not to reveal who he is. John's telling of the gospel makes it abundantly clear who Jesus is, limning not just the man who lived in Galilee and wept at the death of his friend, but stripping away the veil so that we might see the glorified Son who feeds us now and forever. "Amen,

amen, I say to you, . . . I AM." He is the Way, the Truth, and the Life. See him as man, but know that he is God.

As we approach Holy Week, I need to keep before me what John is at such pains to point out. This man, who I can so clearly imagine pacing the temple precincts in a Jerusalem winter to stay warm, and cooking fish for his disciples on the shores of the Sea of Tiberius, is God from God. Indeed, we nailed God to a cross.

Meditation: Which ordinary details about Jesus' life and ministry do you find most compelling? Which details bring home for you that this man, who shivered in the cold and hungered as we do, is God?

Prayer: Jesus, your strength sustains us when we falter, bearing us up, making of us a holy people. Help us to see that you are truly God in the flesh.

Stones Before the Lord

Readings: Jer 20:10-13; John 10:31-42

Scripture:
I love you, O LORD, my strength,
O LORD, my rock, my fortress, my deliverer. (Ps 18:2)

Reflection: The crowd reaches for rocks, to stone Jesus for who he is. The psalmist reaches for stones, too, so we might say who Jesus is: "my rock," "my fortress," "my stronghold," "my rock of refuge."

Rock can be a sanctuary from the heat, or what is thrown in red-hot anger. A stronghold to retreat to in the hills, a fortress on the sea, or a threat hanging above us. A rock is what that rock does.

You wonder who I am, what sort of rock I am? asks Jesus. Look at what I do; look at my deeds:

I can anoint a man's eyes with mud and he can see. I am Light.
I can say to a man who cannot move, "get up and walk." I am the Way.
I can stand in front of a crowd, declare I am the Son of God, and walk through, unharmed. I am the Truth.
I can say, Lazarus, come out, and my friend lives. I am Life.

Build the stronghold of your faith upon this rock, the rock of our salvation. The Way, the Truth, and the Life. God from God. Light from Light.

Meditation: What are the rocks that your faith is built on? What sort of stronghold are you seeking in God? How does God's strength appear in your life, and in what ways are you a foothold for Christ in the world?

Prayer: God, who is our rock, strengthen the foundations of our faith, anchor us in the truth, and shelter us with your life. Make of us a foothold in the world for your son.

Standing at the Edge

Readings: Ezek 37:21-28; John 11:45-56

Scripture:
My dwelling shall be with them;
  I will be their God, and they shall be my people.
    (Ezek 37:27)

Reflection: Tomorrow we enter Holy Week, remembering and celebrating the great sweep of events that led to our salvation, but today's gospel brings to mind the ordinariness of the days that led up to the passion. Mary of Bethany had visitors; Jesus and his disciples spent time talking and praying in a small town on the edge of the desert; there is (as always) strategizing and power-mongering going down in the Sanhedrin; people are getting ready for the holidays and hoping for some extra excitement when they come to the city. Will they see this Jesus of Nazareth?

As I come to the end of Lent, standing on the cusp of the Triduum, I am stopping to take stock of where I am and what I am doing. Am I among the busybodies, whispering about Jesus, scheming to hang on to power? Am I one of the worried and wearied travelers to Jerusalem hoping for a bit of distraction from my earthly concerns? Have I gone to visit Mary and Martha, to see with my own eyes Lazarus raised from the dead? Or am I sitting on a cool rooftop in Ephraim, drinking in the words of Jesus of Nazareth?

Where I stand as the passion is proclaimed depends on where I am standing now in these ordinary moments. It colors how I hear the history of salvation recounted as the church sits in vigil. Will I see Jesus of Nazareth risen from the dead in the garden on Easter morning, or will I brush past the gardener standing by the tree?

Where I stand before the judgment seat of God depends, too, on where I go, what I do, and who I am with in my ordinary days. Will I see Jesus of Nazareth, Son of God, enthroned in glory?

Meditation: As the long season of Lent turns toward Holy Week and Easter, stop with God to take stock of where you have been. Where has your heart been opened? What Scriptures have spoken to you most clearly? What are you still clinging to that you wish to leave behind?

Prayer: Where do we stand with you today, O God? Set us on the path to Holy Week, with our eyes open to see you and our hearts ready to receive you.

Make Holy the Small Things

Readings:
The Blessing and Procession of Palms: Mark 11:1-10 or
    John 12:12-16
The Liturgy of the Word: Isa 50:4-7; Phil 2:6-11; Mark 14:1–15:47
    or Mark 15:1-39

Scripture:
"Why has there been this waste of perfumed oil?
It could have been sold for more than three hundred days'
    wages
    and the money given to the poor." (Mark 14:4a-5b)

Reflection: Seventy-five thousand people in my county do
not always have enough to eat. I think about it each time I
grocery shop, as staples for the food cupboard are standard
on my list, a tithe of my grocery cart for the hungry: five
pounds of rice, tuna fish, cereal, coffee. When I pack it up
each week to take to church I sometimes hear the dinner
guests in Bethany murmuring, *seventy-five thousand hungry
people—do you think what you are doing makes any difference?*

We are engulfed by the passion in Holy Week; it seems a
long way from Ash Wednesday, when the ground was hard
and cold and the branches stuck out like bones. Against that
stark backdrop, the call to justice sounded clearly, but now
that the trees are misted green with new leaves, it gets harder
to imagine that people around me are still cold and hungry.

In the glory and the chaos of Holy Week it's easy to let the everyday work of the gospel become submerged.

But listen, I hear the gospel say, don't let the enormity of what is happening overtake you; pay attention to the people on the edges of the action. Watch the disciples in the garden and the women at the cross, called to companion and witness. Hear the centurion, driven to cry aloud a newfound faith. Feel the weight of the body of Christ, like Simon the Cyrene and Joseph of Arimathea. None of these acts were enough to save Jesus, but all of them made a difference.

What will happen when this week is over? Will I return to the everyday, dropping the faded lilies on the compost heap on the way out? I wonder what happened to Simon the Cyrene and to Salome. The gospels are silent, but somehow I suspect that whatever they went home to, it was never quite ordinary again.

Meditation: In the early church, the days and weeks after baptism at the Easter Vigil were a time of mystagogy, a period during which the newly baptized could begin to see how the mysteries of the faith played out in their lives. As the end of the Lenten season approaches, ask yourself how God is leading you into Easter, what ordinary things have been transformed into sacramental action.

Prayer: Strip us of our pretensions, God, so that we might always walk with your son. Hold us upright, so that we might ever bear his cross. Steady our gaze, so that we might see his suffering in the people around us. Make holy the small things we do in Christ's name.

To Ease the Bruised

Readings: Isa 42:1-7; John 12:1-11

Scripture:
   [He] shall bring forth justice to the nations,
Not crying out, not shouting,
   not making his voice heard in the street. (Isa 42:1b-2)

Reflection: God came wordless to the earth, as a babe. Wordless he will go out of this world, too, if only for a heartbeat. He will not tolerate violence at his arrest, nor will he defend himself before Pilate; there will be no sermon from the cross. No more will he cry out, no longer will he shout, and no more will he make "his voice heard in the street." In this sudden silence, what do I hear?

I hear in the first reading from Isaiah that God, who created us in his image and with his likeness, grasps us by the hand. He sets us aflame as a light to the peoples. Not by our words, but by what we do. In a treatise on the final coming of Christ, Hippolytus, a theologian and martyr of the third century, made clear that this invitation is for everyone. God does not seek his saints and servants among any particular group, does not care whether we are rich or poor, whether we are ignorant or wise, or what country we come from. All of us given breath and spirit by God are worthy to be pulled into the one perfect Body, Christ.

If the Lord is our refuge and salvation, then we must be each other's refuge as well. If the Lord is our light, we must be created to be light, so that those whose vision is dimmed can see clearly, and that we might reach down into the darkness to pull prisoners out from their dungeons. We are to ease the bruised reed, and shelter the flames that are flickering. We must be stouthearted; we must have courage. We are to be the justice that God brings forth to the nations.

Meditation: Find a place to stop and listen; it can be a quiet chair or a noisy street corner. What do you see around you? Can you see smoldering embers in souls you could shelter until they spring brightly to life, or bruised spirits that you could ease?

Prayer: God, you have given us breath and life, you have formed us, and you have taken us by the hand. Now grant us the courage to pour out what we have been given for those who need your tender care. Keep us steadfast in the face of injustice.

Walking with Eyes Open

Readings: Isa 49:1-6; John 13:21-33, 36-38

Scripture:
"Will you lay down your life for me?
Amen, amen, I say to you, the cock will not crow
   before you deny me three times." (John 13:38)

Reflection: For thirty years I've walked a circular route through my neighborhood. My feet know the way and, once begun, I can walk without thinking and sometimes without seeing. But if I remember to look as I walk, there is always something new to see. A tree branch that has fallen, or a young hawk tracing circles over the school field.

I worry that I come to these readings, as I often do to my walk, thinking that I know the ground so well that I can listen with half an ear. But if I stop and listen with full attention, there is always something new in front of me. I see Peter, sitting at that first eucharistic table, formed by his time at Christ's side, ready to follow Jesus. I hear myself in his words, re-formed by this Lenten journey with Christ, "I will lay down my life for you"! But Jesus tells us both, Not so fast!

I don't want to think about sin at the end of a time of penitence, about the certainty that, like Peter, I will again deny Christ, if not in word, then in deed. But I hear Jesus saying, hold on, for all that you desire to follow me, remember you are human, imperfect. You may deny me three times in the next few hours, perhaps even before you get out of the driveway to go to work.

But the psalm today reminds me that wherever I am, walking closely with Christ, or cowering in the darkness around the edges denying that I know him, or somewhere in between, God is at work in the world and in me. I have only to open my eyes and look.

Meditation: Where are the situations where you are most uncomfortable saying you are a follower of Christ? Imagine what Christ might say to you, what strengths he might point out that you have, and what weaknesses he would be tender with.

Prayer: We put our lives in your hands, O God; do not let us be put to shame. Rescue us from our weaknesses, so that we may follow Christ to the end of our lives and beyond.

Flung Forth

Readings: Isa 50:4-9a; Matt 26:14-25

Scripture:
Morning after morning
   he opens my ear that I may hear. (Isa 50:5b)

Reflection: We return each year to the church's celebration of Holy Week, like a comet orbiting the sun. We circle around the passion, death, and glorious resurrection of Christ. Each time we encounter the liturgies of this week, we are burnt and burnished. Morning after morning, day after day, our ears are opened. Each year, we are brought close to the fiery furnace that is the passion, only to be slung out again into Ordinary Time. Each time we approach the risen Christ, a bit of the ice and the stone in our hearts is turned to vapor by the flames, streaming out before us like a sign in the sky for all to see. Mercy is ours. Salvation has been visited upon all the peoples. We come again and again until we are emptied out, like Christ on the cross.

   Poet Rainer Maria Rilke alludes to this tension between our proximity to God and the force with which he propels us into the world in one of the poems collected in *The Book of Pilgrimage*. We are held close in this cycle of liturgies, cradled within the Word made flesh in the readings and at the eucharistic table, perhaps never closer than in these sacred days. Yet even now—as we are about to be closed into our churches in vigil, to listen intently to the story of our salvation, to stretch out our hands between heaven and earth on the altar in remembrance of what Christ did for us—we are poised to be spun out into the world.

As Isaiah reminds us in the first reading, our ears have been opened this Lent, and we have not rebelled; we have not turned back. We have walked to the edge of glory, so that we might be set on fire and sent out once again.

Meditation: Can you think of a time when you knew you were cradled in God's hands, warmed in the light of his face? A time when God's hands flung you out?

Prayer: Cradle us in your Word, O Lord, and sustain us in the vigil to come. Grant us the strength and courage to go forth once again from this season of penance into the light of Easter, and all the ordinary days to come.

Fast Food

Readings: Exod 12:1-8, 11-14; 1 Cor 11:23-26; John 13:1-15

Scripture:
My vows to the LORD I will pay
  in the presence of all his people. (Ps 116:18)

Reflection: "This is how you are to eat it: / with your loins girt, sandals on your feet and your staff in hand, / you shall eat like those who are in flight." We celebrate today the institution of the Eucharist. Exodus reminds us we are not to settle into our pews, to watch events unfold like an epic movie in which the hero rises in the very last scene, only to pour back out into the lobby at intermission, tossing our crumpled worship aids into the recycling bins. No, sit on the edge of your seats, and be ready to fly forth with only what you have in hand.

The Eucharist is fast food, trail food. This is not a private feast, a family dinner to be lingered over, however reverent and beautiful the liturgy is. This is a public meal, food for those in flight, food for those about to be dispatched on a mission. We eat this bread with whoever comes; we drink this cup with all the faithful. We do this with the intent that it will not just fortify us, but change us, so that we might, as St. Augustine counseled, "Be what you see, and receive what you are."

Tonight we will do as Jesus commanded at the Last Supper. We will wash each other's feet, to show each other in the presence of all the faithful what we have vowed to do. We promised at our baptism to be clothed in Christ. So now, we wrap Christ around us, and kneel before the hungry child, the homeless mother, the refugee whose shoes are worn through, to care tenderly for what the world would trample underfoot. We watch that we might become what we see. We eat and drink to receive what we are.

Meditation: What vows have you made to the Lord this Lent? Where do you imagine he might send you, as he sent the disciples with only their staffs and an extra tunic?

Prayer: May we become what we receive, Lord, in your Word and in your sacrament. May we wrap you as a belt around our waists, ready to fly forth at your command.

Listen to the World

Readings: Isa 52:13–53:12; Heb 4:14-16; 5:7-9; John 18:1–19:42

Scripture:
Who would believe what we have heard? (Isa 53:1a)

Reflection: The verse before today's reading of St. John's account of the passion comes from St. Paul's letter to the Philippians and begins, "Christ became obedient to the point of death . . . " Obedience comes from the Latin to listen, to turn your ear toward, *ob audire*. Christ obedient unto death is Christ listening for the will of his Father. Silent, as Isaiah prophesied of the Suffering Servant to come, his face turned toward our salvation.

I think of the ruins of the tiny sixth-century chapel on Inis Caoil, a small island off the Irish coast. I waded out to the island one morning and laid my breviary on what was once the base of the altar to pray Morning Prayer, remembering as I did the monk Connell and the poet Dallan, killed by marauders in 596 CE, saints both, buried beneath its walls. I imagine the monks in the church the night St. Dallan was slain, straining to listen over the howling winds and crashing seas for the creak of oars or snapping of a sail that heralds a boat. What is coming? Life or death?

Like the long-dead Irish monks, we are a people keeping vigil now. Let us turn our ears toward these readings. What do we hear stirring, not just within the witnesses to the passion, but within ourselves? Not just within these walls, but within the wider world? What is coming? The choice stands before us now, set out for us the very first week of Lent. "I have set before you life and death." Bend your ear, listen, and choose life.

Meditation: What line strikes you in the readings? What detail emerges from the chaos? What do you think God is saying to you, today, now, this year? How might you respond? What life do you choose now, at the end of this holy season of Lent?

Prayer: Still us, Lord, so that we might listen to what is stirring within us. Quiet us, Lord, so that we might listen to what is stirring outside of us.

Wracked on Hope's Edge

Readings: Gen 1:1–2:2 or 1:1, 26-31a; Gen 22:1-18 or 22:1-2, 9a, 10-13, 15-18; Exod 14:15–15:1; Isa 54:5-14; Isa 55:1-11; Bar 3:9-15, 32–4:4; Ezek 36:16-17a, 18-28; Rom 6:3-11; Mark 16:1-7

Scripture:
[S]o shall my word be
   that goes forth from my mouth;
my word shall not return to me void,
   but shall do my will,
   achieving the end for which I sent it. (Isa 55:11)

Reflection: The rubrics for the Liturgy of the Word for to-night's Easter Vigil require that enough readings be used so that the celebration retains the character of a vigil. Vigils must be long, the text seems to imply. Yet, the word vigil comes from the Latin meaning "awake," not "long."

Two years ago, when my son, Chris, was a freshman in college three thousand miles from home, he became very ill, ending up in the hospital. Unable to travel to be with him, I spent the night awake, texting him and talking to him on the phone, praying. Keeping vigil. Never far from my thoughts was the Holy Thursday night vigil that had ended in the death of my first husband.

I was awake that night with Chris, not just in the sense of not sleeping, but awake to the fears that batter at hearts in those moments, imagining the demons the Desert Fathers encountered at night fluttering outside the dark windows. Would Chris be all right? Would I have to face searing grief again? But I was awake to hope as well, welling up in my heart at each report.

The character of a vigil is not its length, or its inconvenient time. To keep this Easter vigil means to be awake to the possibility that we will be pushed into spaces we would not willingly go, all the while waiting on hope. We sit in darkened churches, the scent of candles lingering in the air, dressed in Easter finery. Our ears are already straining to hear of glory and grace as we race through millennia of salvation history. But I tell you, now when I sit with the story of Isaac and Abraham, contemplating a son in mortal danger, I am not wrapped in the warmth of a shared history, sure in the knowledge that soon Glorias will ring out, but instead sitting vigil with a wracked Abraham in the desert. Aware he was walking a path he would not have chosen, attuned not to the certainty of a heavenly hosanna, but ears stretched to the limit, hoping to hear God's merciful word. Obedient.

We wait in hope. This is the vigil I am keeping this night, wracked on the edge of hope to the very end.

Meditation: What do you keep vigil for tonight? What do you hope to find? What are you afraid to hope for?

Prayer: Keep us awake, Lord, ever obedient to your Word. Be our hope in these dark hours, our surety in difficult times.

Alleluia!

Readings: Acts 10:34a, 37-43; Col 3:1-4 or 1 Cor 5:6b-8; John 20:1-9 or Mark 16:1-7 or Luke 24:13-35

Scripture:
I shall not die, but live,
  and declare the works of the LORD. (Ps 118:17)

Reflection: While Handel's "Hallelujah Chorus" with its glittering brass glissades and pounding drums may be the iconic grand Easter chorus, for me it is Eric Whitacre's lush and complex choral setting of the single word "Alleluia" that sings of the resurrection. The chorus begins so softly, I'm never sure quite when the piece begins, or if that breath of an alleluia is only in my mind. Soon the alleluias swell and fade in waves. At last the sopranos hit a note almost impossibly high, swirling over the rest until a tenor solo breaks in. *Alleluia.* This is how I imagine the resurrection—Jesus taking that first uncertain breath, his chest barely rising and falling, his breathing gradually growing in strength and regularity, until the Spirit breathes onto him, calling his voice forth again. *Alleluia.* This is the resurrection as I imagine it. No trumpets, no great beams of light, simply God breathing unto God in one unbroken line of praise. *Alleluia.* He is risen. *Alleluia.* We are risen. *Alleluia.* You will rise again. *Alleluia, alleluia,* an infinity of alleluias.

Saint John of the Cross, expanding on his *Spiritual Canticle*, writes of the soul "catching its breath in God." God breathes into us, fashioning us in the image and likeness of the Trinity. We breathe that same air of love back into God. To use Gerard Manley Hopkins's powerful image from his poem "Easter Communion," we who have kept vigil are now breathing Easter, catching our breath again in the resurrection, brought to life from Lent's ashes.

We breathe in to live, we breathe out to speak, to sing, to pray. It is an ordinary miracle we have been given. No trumpets, no gold-clad angelic choruses descending to earth, but simply God's breath ever in our mouths, God's breath ever in our souls. Let us, ever and always, breathe Easter. Alleluia. Alleluia!

Meditation: Imagine what the resurrection might have sounded like to you. Is there a piece of music that captures that sense you could listen to? What might the Trinity have said to each other in that moment? How might you breathe Easter in the next weeks, in your ordinary days?

Prayer:
Breathe in me, O Holy Spirit, that my thoughts may all be holy.
Act in me, O Holy Spirit, that my work, too, may be holy.
Draw my heart, O Holy Spirit, that I love but what is holy.
Strengthen me, O Holy Spirit, to defend all that is holy.
Guard me, then, O Holy Spirit, that I always may be holy.
   (St. Augustine of Hippo)

References

February 15: Thursday after Ash Wednesday
Pope Francis, *Evangelii Gaudium*, The Joy of the Gospel (Vatican City: Libreria Editrice Vaticana, 2013), 191.

February 17: Saturday after Ash Wednesday
Antonio Spadaro, SJ, "A Big Heart Open to God," *America* 209, no. 8 (September 30, 2013): 15.

February 19: Monday of the First Week of Lent
Gerard Manley Hopkins, "As kingfishers catch fire," in *Mortal Beauty, God's Grace: Major Poems and Spiritual Writings of Gerard Manley Hopkins* (New York: Vintage, 2003), 23.

February 24: Saturday of the First Week of Lent
W. S. Gilbert, "I've made a little list," March 10, 2007, *Gilbert & Sullivan Parody*, http://www.jeliza.net/parody/the-mikado/ive-made-a-little-list/.

Madeleine L'Engle, *The Genesis Trilogy: And It Was Good, A Stone for a Pillow, Sold Into Egypt* (Colorado Springs, CO: Shaw Books, 2001), 292.

February 26: Monday of the Second Week of Lent
John Wortley, trans., *The Book of the Elders: Sayings of the Desert Fathers: The Systematic Collection*, Cistercian Studies Series 240 (Collegeville, MN: Cistercian Publications, 2012), 230.

February 27: Tuesday of the Second Week of Lent
Lectionary for Mass: For Sundays of Year A (Washington, DC: Confraternity of Christian Doctrine, 1990).

Rowan Williams, *The Wound of Knowledge: Christian Spirituality from the New Testament to Saint John of the Cross* (Cambridge, MA: Cowley Publications, 2003), 11.

February 28: Wednesday of the Second Week of Lent
Karl Rahner, "On the Experience of Grace," in *Spiritual Writings*, ed. Philip Endean (Maryknoll, NY: Orbis Books, 2004), 75–80.

March 4: Third Sunday of Lent
Demi, *One Grain of Rice: A Mathematical Folktale* (New York: Scholastic Press, 1997).

March 5: Monday of the Third Week of Lent
John O'Donohue, *To Bless the Space between Us: A Book of Blessings* (New York: Doubleday, 2008), 126.

March 7: Wednesday of the Third Week of Lent
Thomas J. Heffernan, *The Passion of Perpetua and Felicity* (New York: Oxford University Press, 2012), 125–36.

March 13: Tuesday of the Fourth Week of Lent
John Chrysostom, Homily 50, in *The Liturgy of the Hours*, Saturday of the Twenty-First Week in Ordinary Time.

March 16: Friday of the Fourth Week of Lent

Alfred Delp and Thomas Merton, *Alfred Delp, S.J.: Prison Writings* (Maryknoll, NY: Orbis Books, 2004), 21.

Mary Frances Coady, *With Bound Hands: A Jesuit in Nazi Germany: The Life and Selected Prison Letters of Alfred Delp* (Chicago: Jesuit Way, 2003), 183.

March 20: Tuesday of the Fifth Week of Lent

See an image of the harrowing of Hades in Istanbul: Chora Museum, "Parecclesion," http://kariye.muze.gov.tr/en/museum/collections/outer-narthex-mosaics/parecclesion_65.html.

March 21: Wednesday of the Fifth Week of Lent

Karl Rahner, *Everyday Faith* (New York: Herder & Herder, 1968), 190.

March 26: Monday of Holy Week

Hippolytus, *Treatise on Christ and Antichrist* II.3.

March 28: Wednesday of Holy Week

Rainer Maria Rilke, *Rilke's Book of Hours: Love Poems to God* (New York: Riverhead Books, 2005), 122.

March 29: Holy Thursday (Maundy Thursday)

Augustine of Hippo, *Sermon 272*, in *Augustine and the Catechumenate*, rev. ed., William Harmless, 376 (Collegeville, MN: Liturgical Press, 2014).

Easter Sunday: The Resurrection of the Lord
Eric Whitacre, "Alleluia" from *Water Night*, Decca, 2012; 3:27 in https://www.youtube.com/watch?v=0JaiSGAZfW4.

Eugene F. Rogers Jr., ed., "St John of the Cross, from 'The Inhalation of the Air,' in The Spiritual Canticle," in *The Holy Spirit: Classic and Contemporary Readings* (Chichester, UK: John Wiley & Sons, 2009), 278–79.